W9-CSN-811

Celebrity Biographies

Taylor Swift

MUSIC SUPERSTAR

BY JEFF BURLINGAME

Enslow Publishers, Inc.
40 Industrial Road
Box 398
Berkeley Heights, NJ 07922
USA
http://www.enslow.com

Library of Congress Cataloging-in-Publication Data:

Burlingame, Jeff.
   Taylor Swift : music superstar / Jeff Burlingame.
     p. cm. — (Hot celebrity biographies)
   Includes index.
   Summary: "Read about Taylor's early life in Pennsylvania, how she got her recording contract, and her life and charity work"—Provided by publisher.
   ISBN 978-0-7660-3870-7
   1. Swift, Taylor, 1989—Juvenile literature. 2. Women country musicians—United States—Biography—Juvenile literature. I. Title.
   ML3930.S989B87 2011
   782.421642092—dc22
   [B]
                        2010048146

Paperback ISBN 978-1-59845-286-0

Printed in the United States of America

052011 Lake Book Manufacturing, Inc., Melrose Park, IL

10 9 8 7 6 5 4 3 2 1

To Our Readers: We have done our best to make sure all Internet addresses in this book were active and appropriate when we went to press. However, the author and the publisher have no control over and assume no liability for the material available on those Internet sites or on other Web sites they may link to. Any comments or suggestions can be sent by e-mail to comments@enslow.com or to the address on the back cover.

♻ Enslow Publishers, Inc., is committed to printing our books on recycled paper. The paper in every book contains 10% to 30% post-consumer waste (PCW). The cover board on the outside of each book contains 100% PCW. Our goal is to do our part to help young people and the environment too!

Photo Credits: AP Photo/Chris Pizzello, p. 1; AP Images/Dan Steinberg, p. 35; AP Images/Donald Traill, p. 36; AP Images/Eric Jamison, p. 19 AP Images/Evan Agostini, pp. 29, 41; AP Images/Jae C. Hong, p. 11; AP Images/Jason DeCrow, p. 27; AP Images/Mark Humphrey, pp. 7, 9, 18; AP Images/Mark J. Terrill, p. 25; AP Images/Matt Sayles, p. 16; AP Images/Peter Kramer, pp. 20, 30; AP Images/Richard Drew, pp. 4, 15, 39; AP Images/Tammie Arroyo, p. 33; PR NEWSWIRE/Newscom, p. 43.

Cover Photo: AP Images/Chris Pizzello (Taylor Swift with her award for Entertainer of the Year at the 46th Annual Academy of Country Music Awards.)

Contents

Taylor Made

Best. First. Youngest. Each time Taylor Swift's name comes up in a newspaper, magazine, or online article, there is a good chance at least one of those three words will be included. Best-selling artist of the year. First country musician to win an MTV Video Music Award. Youngest person in history to win the Grammy award for Album of the Year.

The list goes on.

By the age of twenty-one, she has sold more records than most famous musicians three times her age. She has won more awards than most of those people, too. Along the way, she has become one of the richest celebrities in the world.

In spite of her successes, Swift has managed to remain the same down-to-earth girl she always has been. She often sings about her life. Her fans relate to her songs of hope and heartbreak. They try to figure out who she is singing about. Her lyrics are fairly direct, so that often makes it easy for them to do so.

◀ *Taylor Swift performs on the* Today *show on October 26, 2010.*

"Every single one of the guys that I've written songs about has been tracked down on MySpace by my fans," Swift said. While such lack of privacy might bother some people—especially those being written about—Swift prides herself on being open about her life. That openness is a huge reason why people like her. It is what she expects from a performer so it's what she gives to her fans. "When I knew something was going on in someone's personal life and they didn't address it in their music, I was always very confused by that," she said.

There is no reason for Swift's fans to ever be as confused as she was. She does sing about her personal life. But there is much more to the superstar's story than can be found in her lyrics. It all began with a young girl who had a big dream.

WHO IS TAYLOR SWIFT?
Taylor Alison Swift was born December 13, 1989, in Wyomissing, Pennsylvania. Her parents, Andrea and Scott, both worked in the financial industry. Andrea soon left her career behind to be a stay-at-home mom. However, Scott continued his work as a stockbroker.

Singing appeared to have come naturally to Taylor. Her grandmother was an opera singer. "I can remember her singing, the thrill of it," Taylor told the *Reading Eagle* newspaper in 2008. "She was one of my first inspirations."

Young Taylor also had other musical heroes. They came from a variety of musical styles. She enjoyed the country music of teenager LeAnn Rimes. She also enjoyed older stars such as the Dixie Chicks, Dolly Parton, and Patsy Cline. Even rock and roll music had a place in Taylor's home, thanks to her mom's love of the British rock band Def Leppard. Years later, Taylor Swift got the chance

▼ *At the Country Music Television Awards on June 16, 2009, Taylor Swift got to sing with one of her idols, Def Leppard's Joe Elliott.*

to perform with Def Leppard in concert. When asked about how it felt, she called it "a complete out-of-body experience."

Taylor loved to sing, but she also liked acting and writing. She even performed in a children's acting group. Because she was tall, she landed many lead roles, including Sandy in the musical *Grease*. Taylor also loved reading poetry and began writing it at an early age. In fourth grade, she won a national poetry contest for a three-page poem she wrote. It was titled "Monster in My Closet." "Poetry was my favorite thing," Taylor said. "I loved putting things down on paper. It was so fascinating to me."

EARLY SONGWRITING ADVENTURES

Soon, Taylor's poetry writing turned into songwriting. She began performing hers and others' songs everywhere. She sang at baseball games, county fairs, and karaoke contests. At home, she was always singing. At age eleven, Taylor and her family took a trip to Nashville, Tennessee. Nashville is a city with a strong connection to country music. Taylor was not there to visit. She was there to work.

At the city's many record label offices, she dropped off a homemade demo CD of her singing karaoke. She said, "My mom would pull up outside one of the record labels on Music Row in Nashville and I would run in and say to the receptionist, 'Hi, I'm Taylor. I'm 11. I want a record deal. Call me.'" No one called her—at least not yet.

Rejection did not stop Taylor from following her dream of becoming a star. Instead, she worked harder to achieve her goal. At age twelve, she sang the national anthem at the U.S. Open tennis tournament in New York. She taught herself to play guitar, and practiced for hours each day. She also continued performing near her home. One of her regular shows in public was at a weekly karaoke event in the nearby city of Strausstown. Still twelve, she

▲ Tourists love to visit Music Row in Nashville. Above, a tour bus drives through the intersection of Music Square East and Chet Atkins Place. The Curb Records building is in the background.

TEN TAYLOR FAVORITES

1. Sweet potato casserole at Del Frisco's restaurants.
2. The number thirteen. She was born on December 13 and turned 13 on a Friday the 13th.
3. Dressing girly. Taylor loves to wear dresses and skirts, and often pairs them with cowboy boots.
4. Social media. Taylor's fans can follow her every move because she is constantly keeping them up to date on her Web site, MySpace, Facebook, and Twitter.
5. Sweet desserts, including cookie dough ice cream and cheesecake.
6. The thought of being a mom. In the future, of course.
7. The color white.
8. Christmas.
9. Honesty.
10. The romantic comedy *Love Actually*.

opened up for country music legend Charlie Daniels Band at the Pat Garrett Roadhouse in Strausstown.

ESCAPING WITH MUSIC

Throughout her tween and teen years, Taylor used music as an escape. At school, she said some kids would make fun of her for liking county music because they did not like it. So Taylor would write songs about those experiences to help her cope. "I didn't really have that many friends at school," she said.

It just dawned on me that I had to love being different or else I was going to end up being dark and angry and frustrated by school. I would sit on the edge of class and watch people interact with each other. I'd watch guys flirt with cool girls and I would watch best friends talk, and I would go home and write about it. If you listen to my albums, it's like reading my diary.

One of Taylor's earliest songs was called "The Outside." It was written about not being one of the crowd and being "on the outside looking in."

The roughly eight hundred miles between Taylor's home in Wyomissing and Nashville did not stop the family from visiting there often. They visited the city so Taylor could work with songwriters there. During the summer before Taylor's freshman year of high school, the Swifts—mom, dad, Taylor, and her younger brother, Austin—decided to make that trip a lot easier. That is when they moved to Hendersonville, Tennessee. The suburb was just twenty minutes away from Nashville. Taylor's father moved his business to Nashville in order to help his daughter succeed. It was one of the many sacrifices Taylor's parents made for their daughter over the years.

Later that year, when Taylor was fourteen, she was invited to play a few songs for RCA Records. The label liked them, and signed Taylor to a development deal. That meant RCA would watch Taylor for a year and see how she grew as a songwriter and a performer. She and her family agreed to do it. But at the end of the year, RCA decided it was not ready to sign Taylor to a record deal. "They wanted to shelf me," she said, "keep me in development till I was probably about eighteen. So I walked away from the biggest record label in Nashville."

Taylor believed she was ready for stardom right away. She did not want to wait until she was eighteen. In no time, she proved herself right.

Journey to the Top

Ending her development deal with RCA Records did not stop Taylor. Instead, she became even more determined to succeed. Soon, she signed a publishing deal with Sony/ATV Music. The deal made Taylor a staff songwriter for the company. She was still fourteen years old, which made her the youngest person ever to have this job.

She also did some modeling, and appeared in the Fall 2004 Abercrombie & Fitch "Rising Stars" catalog. Other future stars featured in the catalog included actresses Michelle Trachtenberg, Nikki Reed, and Poppy Montgomery.

Taylor continued playing her songs wherever she could. At one event her dreams of becoming a star came closer to coming true. It was at a songwriting showcase at Nashville's famous Bluebird Café. When she was done with her songs, Taylor was approached by a man named Scott Borchetta.

He wanted to sign her to a contract with a record label he was creating. It was called Big Machine Records. Borchetta later said that was because he had fallen in love with Taylor's performance. "I remember sitting there just [wondering] is this gonna hit me? And it absolutely did.

And so I went and met with the family after that." The family agreed to a deal with Borchetta. Doing so was a big risk because his company was so new. Taylor was the first artist he had signed. But the risk paid off. Success was right around the corner.

DISCOVERING "TIM McGRAW"

Borchetta believed he was onto something with his new employee. But he did not know exactly how big she could become. At least that was the case until August 2005. That's when the then-fifteen-year-old played him a new song she had written during her high school math class.

The song was called "Tim McGraw," after the country music star of the same name. Like many of Taylor's songs, this one was about love. More specifically, it was about her thoughts of what life would be like when she broke up with her current boyfriend. He was a senior in high school and would soon be moving for college. Taylor knew they could not stay together when he left.

When Borchetta heard the song, he knew it would be a hit. Less than a year later, the song was released as Taylor's first single. For fifteen weeks, it was one of the top one hundred country songs in the United States. It eventually rose to as high as number six. More than one million copies of the song were sold.

Taylor's first album was called *Taylor Swift*. It was released in 2006. It was a huge success. Even many hard-to-please critics liked it. The album became the number one country album in the United States. Perhaps even more surprising to many people was the fact that Taylor had written or cowritten each of the eleven songs on the record. It is rare for someone so young to do so. When the album came out, Taylor was only sixteen.

Most of the album's songs were about her life. "The Outside," the song she had written at age twelve, was on there. So was "Our Song," which Taylor had written for a talent show during her freshman year of high school. It was about a boy she was dating at the time. She wrote it

▲ *Taylor's first hit song was about country star Tim McGraw. Here, she poses with McGraw and his wife, singer Faith Hill.*

because the couple did not have their "own" song as many couples do. Taylor's other hit singles included "Teardrops on My Guitar," which was about a boy she knew named Drew; "Picture to Burn"; and "Should've Said No," a song about a boy who cheated on a girl.

A BUDDING STAR

Taylor's life changed a lot in the two years between the 2006 release of "Tim McGraw" and the 2008 release of the final single from her debut album. Now eighteen, Taylor was a rising star not only in the world of country music, but in all of pop culture, too. She had performed in huge stadiums with country legends Kenny Chesney, Rascal Flatts, George Strait, and Brad Paisley. She had played with Tim McGraw and his wife, Faith Hill. She had sold millions of records. She had been nominated for a Grammy award for Best New Artist. Although she did not win that award, she did win several others, including Video of the Year for "Our Song." She had been featured on several magazine covers and performed on many TV shows.

"What surprised me over the past year is that I thought I'd already made it," she told the *Reading Eagle* newspaper in 2008. "That I was in an amazing place where I would be thrilled to stay. I thought, 'I don't need to be any bigger than this to be happy.' But then it just blew up! I'd be lying if I said I had this all planned. I honestly don't know how it happened. It's such a blessing."

SKIPPING SENIOR PROM

Taylor's personal life also saw many twists and turns during this period. She left Henderson High School to be home-schooled. That allowed her to continue her education while she was on tour.

Although she would have been allowed to, she decided not to attend the senior prom at her former school. She did not want to deal with the negative people she thought would bother her if she went to the dance. She said she had some enemies there.

FAMILY SUPPORT

Throughout her life, Taylor's parents played important roles in helping her become a star. The Swifts used their business skills to help their daughter get chances other children might not have been able to get. For example, Scott Swift's contact with an old friend helped Taylor get the chance to sing the national anthem at the 2008 World Series. That performance placed Taylor on a national stage and introduced her to many people who may otherwise not have seen her. Taylor has given her parents credit many times. In fact, she has said her worst fear in life is disappointing them.

◄ *Taylor Swift celebrates with her brother, Austin, after she wins Video of the Year for her song "Love Story" at the Country Music Television Awards on June 16, 2009.*

"As supportive as my hometown is, in my high school, there are people who would probably walk up to me and punch me in the face," she said.

There's a select few that will never like me. They don't like what I stand for. They don't like somebody who stands for being sober, who stands for anything happy. They're going to be negative no matter what. . . . I heard that when Christina Aguilera went back to her prom, people, like, booed her. I can't imagine going through that.

STAYING GROUNDED

Despite the success of her first album, Taylor somehow managed to remain the same humble person she always had been. "I think I've tried as much as possible to stay the same person," she said. "But nothing about my life is the same as it was two years ago. But I'm still the same person. Your schedule can change, but I continue to walk around with the mentality that I'm not really a big deal because as fast as it came, it can go."

It was a good thing Taylor was able to keep her head squarely on her shoulders. Taylor was about to become a superstar. Soon, everyone would know her name.

▲ Taylor Swift holds the award for Top New Female Vocalist, which she won at the Academy of Country Music Awards on May 18, 2008.

Superstardom

Sophomore slump. Those are the words that are used in many areas of life to describe people who achieved early success, but then had a hard time doing it again the second time they tried. In the music industry, the words are used when talking about an artist's second album.

Since Taylor's first album was such a huge hit, many wondered whether she would have a sophomore slump with her new album. Would her fans enjoy her new songs as much as they had her first ones? Would her album sell as well and win as many awards?

The answers—or at least one big clue—actually came two months before the album was released. That is when the song "Love Story" was released to radio stations. Taylor said she wrote the song in twenty minutes on her bedroom floor. But that didn't matter to listeners. "Love Story" quickly became the number one country song in America. The song was a hit on the pop charts, too.

◄ *Taylor Swift received the Song of the Year award at the 2008 BMI Country Awards for "Teardrops on My Guitar." A year later, she won the same award for "Love Story."*

Taylor told *Time* magazine:

> [The song] is actually about a guy that I almost dated. But when I introduced him to my family and my friends, they all said they didn't like him. … For the first time, I could relate to that Romeo-and-Juliet situation where the only people who wanted them to be together were them. That's the most romantic song I've written, and it's not even about a person I really dated.

The song's video was also based on William Shakespeare's story of *Romeo and Juliet*.

DEBUTING ON TOP

Taylor Swift's second album, *Fearless*, was released in November 2008. Thanks in part to the success of "Love Story," the album was an instant smash. Not only did it debut on top of the country charts, but *Fearless* also was the number one album of any style in all of America. It took over the top spot held by the soundtrack to the movie *Twilight*.

Swift's second album was number one for more time than any other album by a female country music artist in history. Soon, other records began to fall, too.

"Love Story" set the record for most paid downloads ever with more than 3 million. Six of the songs on *Fearless* sold well enough to be ranked in the top twenty in the country. That set another record. Those songs included "Love

NOT-SO-TANGLED WEB

Taylor Swift became one of America's biggest stars in 2008 thanks in part to the Internet. She set records for the most streamed videos and was the most searched artist on MySpace with more than 200 million streams of her songs that year. Today, Swift's Facebook account is equally popular. She has 16 million fans on that site, and her frequent updates receive thousands of comments each. She has 5 million fans on Twitter.

Swift uses social media to keep in touch with her fans in other ways, too. On her official Web site, she sometimes hosts live chats. During them, she answers questions asked by her fans. Before one chat in 2010, Swift said, "I've gotten so many questions from fans—on Twitter, Facebook, MySpace, my website, everywhere really ... I can't wait to talk to everybody as directly as I can!"

Story," as well as "White Horse," "You Belong With Me," and "Fifteen." In 2008, Taylor sold more CDs than any other artist in the United States.

As always, Swift did not brag about her popularity. She told *Digital Spy*:

> [W]hen I look at my sales figures I can't take credit for them. I can write songs and sing them and try to make the best [album] possible, but if I put that record out and nobody buys it that's out of my control. I credit my fans for my success. Also, my friends and family haven't changed their

perception of me since all this happened. They tell me when I'm being moody and a brat and make sure I snap out of it.

It was obvious music fans loved Swift's second album—even more than they had the first one. But what about music critics? Turns out, they felt the same way. *Rolling Stone* magazine said Swift's album "sounds like it has been scientifically engineered in a hit factory." The Associated Press asked "When an unknown teenage artist and an upstart label both come from nowhere to sell well over three million albums, the question is: What do you do next? With Taylor Swift's sophomore album *Fearless*, the answer is: You get even better." *Billboard* magazine said "Those who thought Taylor Swift was a big deal after the release of her first [album] should be prepared: She's about to get way bigger."

BLOWING UP

The record-breaking sales and positive reviews opened the door for even bigger performances. At twenty years old, Taylor Swift became the youngest country singer to ever perform on *Saturday Night Live* in January 2009. She also did a little acting on that show and others, including one episode of the drama *CSI*. She then made her feature film debut in the 2010 movie *Valentine's Day*.

Her sales successes allowed her to headline a national tour for the first time. The *Fearless* tour included stops at major venues across the United States. Many of the shows,

Taylor Swift performs at the Academy of Country Music Awards in Las Vegas on April 5, 2009.

including ones in Los Angeles and New York, sold out in less than two minutes. All fifty-two of the shows were sold out more than one month before the tour even began. *Fearless* also won the Grammy award for Album of the Year, in addition to dozens of other awards.

DISSED BY KANYE WEST

Not all of Swift's award-winning experiences have been positive. In fact, one of them was embarrassing. At the 2009 MTV Video Music Awards (VMAs) in New York City, she was onstage accepting the award for Best Female Video when rapper Kanye West stormed onto the stage. Kanye took the microphone from Swift and said he believed singer Beyoncé should have won the award instead.

Swift was stunned and stood by watching. The crowd booed Kanye. Later in the evening, Beyoncé won an award. When she took the stage, she called Swift up, gave her a hug and let her finish the speech that had been interrupted earlier.

The event made headlines and Kanye took a lot of heat for what he did. He later apologized to Swift on Twitter. But during the VMAs one year later, Swift performed a new song called "Innocent." She took a subtle shot at Kanye during the song. Some people were upset with Swift for doing so, especially because the introduction of her performance featured a video of Kanye interrupting her the previous year. People wanted her to forget the incident.

▲ *Kanye West grabs the microphone from a stunned Taylor Swift after she wins Best Female Video at the 2009 MTV Video Music Awards.*

Critics have also taken shots at Taylor Swift for other reasons. They have said her voice is not as good when she performs live as it is when she records it in a studio. They think that the technology used in the studio is what makes Swift sound so good. After Swift received heavy criticism for a performance at the 2010 Grammy Awards, the head of her record label defended her. He said, "She is the voice of

THE MEN IN TAYLOR'S LIFE

Taylor Swift's song lyrics are inspired by events in her life, including romances. She has had some famous boyfriends—such as Joe Jonas of the Jonas Brothers, and Taylor Lautner, the hunky actor who plays Jacob Black in the *Twilight* movie series. Some also say she was romantically linked to singer-songwriter John Mayer.

Shortly after her public split from Jonas, she told radio host Ryan Seacrest, "I've written about (the split), and I like to write about my life ... that's just how I deal with things." She said that she wrote the song "Forever and Always" about the breakup and recorded it at the last minute just to make sure it was put on her second album. She told People.com the song was, "About watching somebody completely fade away in a relationship and wondering what you did wrong." She also posted a MySpace video featuring a Joe Jonas doll. During the video she said, "This one even comes with a phone so it can break up with other dolls!"

On her third album, *Speak Now*, there is a song titled "Back to December." Some believe the lyrics are an apology to former flame Lautner for breaking up with him. In the song, Swift sings about swallowing her pride and how good the boy was to her. On the same album, there is a song called "Dear John" that is rumored to be written about John Mayer. In the song, Swift sings about how she regrets the relationship and how people believed she was crazy for getting into it in the first place.

During the last part of 2010, Swift began dating actor Jake Gyllenhaal. The relationship did not last long. The couple broke up during the first part of 2011.

this generation. She speaks directly to (her fans), and they speak directly back to her. This is not *American Idol*. This is not a competition of getting up and seeing who can sing the highest note. This is about a true artist and writer and communicator."

▲ *John Mayer and Taylor Swift perform at the Z100 Jingle Ball in New York City on December 11, 2009. The two were rumored to have been dating at the time.*

Her Place in the World

Taylor Swift's ability to remain down to earth despite all her successes has shocked many people. One reporter from the *Washington Post* wrote "Why can't they all be like Taylor Swift? The young country super-starlet is a flat-out fantastic interview subject. So open and honest and funny and interesting; so willing to play along … she seems to love the process. And the process sure loves her: She's a reporter's dream." Scott Borchetta, the head of Swift's record label, said he believes media members—and fans—like Taylor Swift because she's real. They can understand what she is writing about because they have the same feelings.

Unlike many stars who have achieved big things, Swift did not allow it to ruin her personal life with vices such as alcohol or drugs. She has remained wholesome. In 2009, she told a *Rolling Stone* magazine writer she had never smoked a cigarette or drank a single drop of alcohol. "I have no interest in drinking," she said. "I want to be

◄ Taylor Swift holds her "moon man" statute for Best Female Video, as she poses for photos after the 2009 MTV Video Music Awards.

DOWN TIME

Taylor's busy schedule does not allow much time for hobbies. But she does enjoy watching TV shows, such as *CSI* and *Law & Order*, on her tour bus. She also likes to go shopping and bake.

responsible for the things I do." She also said, "I have never really been a partier. I'm kind of a big dork. I was always afraid to go to parties because I was afraid people would be drinking and maybe the cops would show up and I couldn't risk it, I just couldn't. Part of who I am, and trying to be a role model is having responsibility."

Keeping busy helps keep her out of trouble. Choosing to continue living in Tennessee does, too. When she is there, Taylor Swift is far away from the mass of paparazzi, or celebrity photographers, that constantly shadow stars in Hollywood, California.

CHARITABLE CAUSES

Even with her busy schedule, Swift has always found time to give back to those less fortunate than she is. In Tennessee in 2007, she began a movement to protect children from online predators. Swift worked with that state's governor to give out Internet safety information to parents and students. Swift told kids they need to be careful because, "when you meet somebody online, you can never really know them." The movement was called Delete Online Predators. Swift also has helped the Red Cross by donating some of her T-shirt sales to the

▲ Taylor Swift sings at a concert to raise money for the Country Music Hall of Fame and Museum. The concert took place at Los Angeles's Club Nokia on September 23, 2010.

charity. St. Jude's Children's Hospital, flood victims in Iowa and Tennessee, various schools across the country, and many other causes have also been helped by Swift.

In January 2010, roughly three hundred thousand people died and more than a million people were either injured or left homeless after an earthquake struck the country of Haiti. Taylor Swift was one of many superstars to perform in a telethon to raise money for victims of the disaster. Swift sang "Breathless." The song was written by the rock band Better Than Ezra, whose hometown of New Orleans, Louisiana, had gone through a similar tragedy in 2005 when a brutal hurricane devastated the city. Others who played during the benefit included Justin Timberlake, Alicia Keys, Mary J. Blige, Madonna, and many more. The benefit was called Hope for Haiti Now: A Global Benefit for Earthquake Relief.

"SPILLOVER ARTIST"

Exactly what genre Taylor Swift's songs fall into is up for debate. Some call her music country. Some call it pop. Swift doesn't call herself either. She calls herself a "spillover artist." By that, she means that her music fills up the country radio stations, and then it spills over onto the pop stations. Then it spills onto stations that play various other forms of music.

Her songs, Swift has said, have such mass appeal because they are about real life. Her stories are personal to her, but she leaves them vague enough so others can picture how the lyrics apply to their lives. She also sticks to basic subjects all her fans can relate to. "I didn't want to write songs about being on the road and being in hotels and missing your family and missing your friends," she said. "When I was like 14 or 15 and I would hear those things on an album ... being alone, living out of a suitcase. And I was always like, 'Ugh, skip!' I'm inspired by boys and love."

▼ *Taylor Swift even plays the drums at some of her concerts.*

Never Holding Back

As the release date of Taylor Swift's third album drew near, her fans grew anxious. Everyone wanted answers. What and who would the new songs be about? What would the album be called? What would the cover look like? Would she be able to continue the remarkable success she had experienced for the past four years? Or was she finally in for a fall?

As *Billboard* magazine said, "[Taylor Swift's new album] could prove to be a pivotal album in Swift's creative progress. Music history is littered with teen stars that were unable to maintain their commercial pace once they hit their 20s. But in most instances, those acts didn't write their own material. Swift penned every song on [the album]—often at odd hours on the road. In the end, that led her to write the entire project without enlisting any co-writers." Once again, whether Taylor Swift sank or swam would mostly be based on how well her fans felt about the personal stories she was telling.

◀ *On October 27, 2010, Taylor Swift performed at the JFK Airport in New York to promote her new album, Speak Now.*

QUESTIONS ANSWERED

Many questions were answered in October 2010. That is when the album, titled *Speak Now*, hit store shelves. The outside of the album featured a photograph of Swift in a sparkly purple dress. The inside featured fourteen songs, each one being "a different confession to a person," Taylor said. "In the past two years, I've experienced a lot of things that I've been dying to write about. A lot of things I wanted to say in the moment that I didn't."

Swift's fourteen stories included the single "Mine." She said it was about her tendency to run away from love every time it comes her way. She did not say exactly who the song was written about. Some have guessed it might be about her relationship with Taylor Lautner, as was "Back to December." Other songs on Swift's new record included the Kanye West-inspired "Innocent," the title song, "Speak Now," and "Better Than Revenge." "Better Than Revenge" is believed to be about the girl who stole Joe Jonas away from her.

As they had with her first two records, critics generally liked *Speak Now*. The *Washington Post* called it "ridiculously entertaining." The *New York Times* said the record was "the most savage of her career, and also the most musically diverse. And it's excellent too, possibly her best." Critics—those who think Taylor Swift can't sing—are even a subject of a song on the new album. "Mean" talks about how Taylor knows what her flaws are musically, so there is no need for anyone to point them out. In addition to the praise it received, *Speak Now* was the best-selling Internet album of 2010. Those sales helped make Swift the top-selling artist of the year in the United States. They also helped make *Speak Now* the number one album in the country for several weeks.

▲ *Taylor Swift and America's Got Talent host Nick Cannon speak to New York City students during the Read Now With Taylor Swift event.*

ENDORSEMENT CHECKS

Most of the money Taylor earns comes directly from her music career—including album and song sales and touring. But a large part of her earnings also comes from agreements she has to promote products outside the music industry. Swift doesn't just make music—she also helps sell sundresses, greeting cards, and milk. Among other deals, Taylor has:

* Worn a "Got Milk" moustache to encourage kids to drink more milk and less soda and other sugary drinks.
* Worn L.E.I. jeans and a white tank top in ads for the brand. She also created sundresses for L.E.I.
* Created a line of cards for American Greetings.
* Been a CoverGirl for the cosmetic company of the same name.

MAKING MILLIONS

Whatever flaws Swift has, none have stopped her from selling records and making tons of money. In 2010, *Forbes* magazine listed her as the twelfth most powerful celebrity in the United States. The magazine said she made $45 million in the previous year. That ranked her higher than many older celebrities on the list, including Miley Cyrus, basketball star Kobe Bryant, and the Jonas Brothers, who were fortieth. Five musicians—Beyoncé, Lady Gaga, Britney Spears, U2, and Madonna ranked above Swift on the list. However, Taylor was the highest-ranked country musician. She was ahead of such legends as Kenny Chesney, Rascal Flatts, Toby Keith, and Keith Urban.

▲ All indications are that Taylor Swift will be a big name in the music scene for a long time to come.

A BRIGHT FUTURE

At twenty-one years old, Taylor Swift said she realized there still are goals left for her to go for. She wants to know if she can become a career artist. Will her image and music change and grow along with her many young fans? Or will those fans grow up and leave her music behind? Could she become a household name in other countries? That is something not many country artists in history have been able to pull off. Her first world tour in 2011 got her off to a good start with that goal. The tour took her to places such as Japan, Italy, Germany, France, Spain, and England.

Critics want to know if she will be able to continue to be the down-to-earth country singer her fans have come to know and love.

According to Swift, that answer is "Yes."

"I want my fans to know I'm the same girl I was when the first album came out," she said. "I'm just not in high school and I have a different schedule. I feel the same things, I feel the same way. And my songs are where I'll never hold back."

In preparation for her 2011 Speak Now *world tour, Taylor Swift* ▶ *performed on a Royal Caribbean cruise ship on January 21, 2011.*

Timeline

1989 Taylor Alison Swift is born in Wyomissing, Pennsylvania, on December 13.

1999 Wins contest for her poem, "Monster in My Closet."

2001 Takes spring break trip with family to Nashville and drops demo CD off at record label offices.

2002 Sings national anthem at U.S. Open tennis tournament.

2003 Signs development deal with RCA Records.

2004 Family moves to Hendersonville, Tennessee, to be closer to Nashville.

2004 Accepts songwriting job with Sony/ATV Music.

2005 Signs record deal with Big Machine Records.

2006 Releases first single, "Tim McGraw."

2006 Self-titled debut album is released.

2007 "Our Song" becomes her first number one single.

2008 Second album, *Fearless*, is released to rave reviews.

2009 Performs on *Saturday Night Live* and at the Grammy Awards ceremony.

2010 Third album, *Speak Now*, is released.

2011 Begins *Speak Now* World Tour in February in Singapore.

Further Info

BOOKS

Hansen, Amy Gail. *Taylor Swift: Secrets of a Songwriter*. Chicago: Triumph Books, 2010.

Ryals, Lexi. *Taylor Swift: Country's Sweetheart*. New York: Price Stern Sloan, 2008.

DVDs

CMT Crossroads: Taylor Swift and Def Leppard, 2009.

Valentine's Day, 2010.

INTERNET ADDRESSES

Taylor Swift's Official Web site
www.taylorswift.com

Taylor Swift's Official MySpace Page
www.myspace.com/taylorswift

Taylor Swift's Record Label
www.bigmachinerecords.com

Discography

ALBUMS
2006 — *Taylor Swift*
2008 — *Fearless*
2010 — *Speak Now*

EPs
2007 — *Sounds of the Season: The Taylor Swift Holiday Collection*
2009 — *Beautiful Eyes*

SELECTED SINGLES
2006 — "Tim McGraw"
2007 — "Teardrops on My Guitar"
       "Our Song"

2008 — "Picture to Burn"
       "Love Story"
       "Change"
       "White Horse"
2009 — "Fifteen"
2010 — "Fearless"
       "Back to December"
       "Mine"
       "Speak Now"
       "Mean"

Glossary

anticipation — Expectation or hope.

demo — An unpublished and often unpolished recording of a musician's work.

endorsements — Approving something, such as a company's product, in exchange for payment from the company.

Grammy — Prestigious award given each year by the National Academy of Recording Arts and Sciences to musicians in a variety of categories.

pop music — Any kind of music that appeals to many people and often has memorable lyrics and music.

record label — A company, or branch of a company, that produces and promotes musical releases.

sophomore — A second effort or a second version of something.

soundtrack — The music from a motion picture or TV show, often released as a CD for commercial purposes.

suburb — A smaller community located outside a larger city or town.

Index

I like school

Bobbie Kalman

The In My World Series

Toronto New York Crabtree Publishing Company

The In My World Series
Conceived and coordinated by Bobbie Kalman

Writing team:
Bobbie Kalman
Diane Cook-Brissenden
Susan Hughes

Editors:
Susan Hughes
Ruth Chernia

Cover and title page design:
Oksana Ruczenczyn, Leslie Smart and Associates

Design and mechanicals:
Ruth Chernia

Illustrations:
Title page by Karen Harrison © Crabtree Publishing Company 1985
Pages 28-32 by Deborah Drew-Brook-Cormack
© Crabtree Publishing Company 1985
Pages 4-27 and cover © Mitchell Beazley Publishers 1982

Cataloging in Publication Data

Kalman, Bobbie, 1947–
   I like school

(The In my world series)
ISBN 0-86505-064-3

1. School environment – Juvenile literature.
I. Title. II. Series.

LB1513.K34 1985   j372.1

To Olivia

350 Fifth Avenue
Suite 3308
New York, N.Y. 10118

102 Torbrick Avenue
Toronto, Ontario
Canada M4J 4Z5

Contents

I am in kindergarten

This is my first year at school.
I go to school all morning.
On the first morning, I was scared. I missed Mom.
Now I like school.
There are lots of fun things to do here.
We sing songs.
The teacher reads us books.
We draw pictures and make up stories.

I can play with all kinds of toys.
Sometimes I have to share the toys
with others, but I don't mind.
Now I have many friends.
I know my friends like playing with the toys too.

I still miss my mom sometimes, but
I like playing with my friends.

We are getting ready to go home now.
Some of my friends know how to
dress themselves.
I can tie up my laces.
I am doing more things by myself now that I am
in school, but I still need help doing up buttons.
My teacher helps me button up my coat.
Soon I will learn how to do up buttons by myself.

School is a place to learn new things.
School is a place to have fun.
I'm glad I am going to school.

Picture talk
Did your life change when you started
going to school? How?
What new things have you learned to do
since you started school?

I go to school all day

My name is Angela.
Last year I was in kindergarten.
I only went to school in the morning.
Now I am in first grade.
I go to school all day.
At first it was hard to be in school all day.
Now I like it.

I like my class because we have first
and second grade children in it.
My friend Paul is in second grade, but
he is in my classroom.

We have math and science in the morning.
We learn how to sort and measure things.
We count and learn to write numbers.
We learn reading and writing in the afternoon.
We sing songs and play music too.

Today Paul and I are learning how to use
the scales.
I am putting blocks on my side of the scales.
Paul is putting coloring pencils on his side.
My blocks are heavier than his pencils.

My teacher and my friend Bobbie are using
blocks to learn about numbers.
Soon my teacher will work with Paul and me.
She shows us how to learn things on our own.

Picture talk

What do you most enjoy doing in school?
What work can you do on your own?
What do you find hard to do on your own?
Can you name the shapes and colors
in the border of this picture?

I love science best!

Science is my favorite subject.
My teacher, Mr. Cormack, doesn't just use
books to teach us.
He brings animals, bugs, and other living
things right into the classroom.
Sometimes my class goes outside
to search for leaves and flowers.

We're learning about snails this week.
Snails are fun because they don't run from us.
Maybe they're just not afraid!
We watch them move slowly.
They always carry their houses on their backs.
Can you imagine carrying your home?

Today Mr. Cormack let us pretend to be snails.
We crawled from one side of the classroom
to the other with heavy knapsacks on our backs.
We got tired very quickly.
I guess we're not as strong as snails are.

Tomorrow our snails will have a race.
We will put leaves in the center of the room.
The snails will be placed so that they are each
the same distance from the leaves.
Then we will cheer our favorite snails
to victory.
What a fun way to learn about snails!

Picture talk

Which snail do you think will win the race?
How are these children learning about snails?
What is the girl on the right looking through?
What is she looking at?

Library time

The best part of school is learning to read.
I go to a small school.
My school does not have a library.
When we want to get books to read, my class
goes down the street to the public library.
I have my own library card.
I can take out any book I want.

Libraries are lots of fun.
They are full of secret treasures.
When I open a book, I might find an exciting
story, some beautiful drawings, or photographs
of children from other countries.
My favorite books are about dinosaurs.

My teacher goes to the library with my class.
She chooses books to read to us during the week.
My teacher likes funny books.
We all laugh when she reads to us.

The library has special rules.
We must speak quietly when we are there.
People like to read in a quiet place.
We must not write in library books.
We have to return the books we borrow.
Sometimes I find a book in the back of my desk.
It is overdue.
I must pay a fine when I take the book
back to the library.
The fine helps me remember to return
my book on time the next time!

Picture talk

Do you have a library at your school?
When do you use it?
What are your favorite books about?

Making music

My name is Ricky.
This is my music class.
Can you see me playing the recorder?
Watch my fingers fly!

Mr. Sandburg is our music teacher.
He shows us how to play the instruments.
1—2—3—4. We are following the rhythm.
Yoli and Tibor are playing the drums.
Mark and Marie are playing the tambourine
and the triangle.
Pam and Mike are playing xylophones.
Karl and Eva are shaking maracas.
The rest of my friends are playing recorders.

We sing songs from all over the world.
When Mr. Sandburg plays the piano or guitar,
we follow the tune.
I can make my voice sing a high note.
I can make my voice sing a low note.

I like singing, but I like playing
the recorder even better.
I would like to play the flute,
but first I must learn to read music.
Maybe one day I can play in the school band.

Picture talk
How many shaking instruments do you see
in the picture and the border?
Which instruments make a sound
when air is blown into them?
Which instruments must be strummed or plucked?
Which instruments have to be tapped or hit?
Which instrument would you like to play?

It's recess

Ralph is my name. Soccer is my game.
I learned to play soccer at school during
my physical education class.
I like to play soccer during recess.

I'm Peter. I am new at this school.
I could skip with my own rope,
but I don't want to.
I would rather play with the other children,
but they didn't ask me to play with them.
I know school is a good place to
make friends, but I'm too shy to tell the kids
that I want to play with them.

I'm Tina. I am waiting for my turn at marbles.
I did not always wait for my turn.
I used to get impatient.
The other kids got angry with me.
I have learned to wait for my turn.
Now my friends and I have fun
when we play marbles.

I'm Elaine. I like recess.
I like to run and jump.
I like to spin and skip.
I'm glad we have recess twice a day!

Picture talk
If you were skipping, would you ask Peter
to join your game?
How would you ask him?
Which children are waiting for a turn?
Why do people have to take turns?
Playing with friends is fun. Playing alone
is also fun. What games do you play by yourself?

My imagination

My imagination makes learning fun.
I can become an animal just as easy as this.
Stomp! Stomp! Stomp!
I can make my body feel heavy.
I am a huge gray elephant with big ears.

I can make my body feel light.
I can pretend to swing and climb and hang.
Now I am a monkey.

I can pretend to glide through the air.
I can stand in the water on one leg.
Did you guess?
I am a pink flamingo.

I use my imagination in other ways too.
Sometimes I pretend I am grown up.
I use my imagination when I draw pictures
or write stories.
My teacher puts a gold star on my work.
She thinks my stories are very good.

My teacher says that having a good
imagination is just as important as being
good at math or reading.
I am glad because I have a great imagination!

Picture talk
Which animals are the children pretending to be?
Which animals can you see on
the classroom walls?
What animals are the children drawing?
How is the boy with the broken arm
using his imagination?
How do you use your imagination?

17

What is art?

Why are we wearing shirts to cover our clothes?
Why are our hands different colors?
When we create, we get messy!

My favorite activity at school is art.
Art is painting. Art is molding.
Art is building. Art is drawing.
Art is making something that is special to me.
I like art because it helps me to show
my ideas.

Nina is making a face.
She presses her fingers into the clay to mold
a mouth and face.
The clay feels squishy!
Jennifer and Amy are building a crocodile.
Have you ever seen such a creature?

I am painting with my fingers.
Morgan is painting with a brush.
Hands, feet, potatoes, and fruit
all become pictures when I dip them
into paint and press them onto paper.

The finished paintings are put on the wall.
I hope the teacher puts up my painting!

Picture talk

What materials are the children using to make
the crocodile?
Which art activity would you choose to do? Why?
Which is your favorite way of painting?
How are some of the children cleaning up?
Why is it important to help clean up?

Field day

We have a physical education class
three times a week.
We run, play games, and do exercises
to music.

Twice a year we have a track and field day
at school.
Everyone in the school goes outside.
We run and jump and throw.
We cheer for one another.

I can run faster and jump farther
this year than I could last year.
I used to cry if I didn't win a race.
Now I don't cry when I lose.
I know I can't win all the time.
I feel good as long as I know
I have tried my best.

My friend Otto is in a wheelchair.
He can't run, but he is learning
to throw the discus.
The coach is teaching Otto exercises
to strengthen the muscles in his arms.

My friend Marie is doing a long jump.
She flies through the air and lands in the sand.
She has been practicing all week.
How far did she jump?

Picture talk

Do you have a field day at your school?
Which is your best sport?
Do you think it is important
to win a race? Why or why not?

Outdoor education

My class went on a hike for the day.
Our teacher and four parents took us to a park.
We walked along trails in the woods.
We saw small animals and many kinds of birds.
We collected leaves of different colors.

We made a path across the stream.
We used stones and logs.
Ed brought his dog Rocky on the hike.
Rocky didn't use our stones and logs
to cross the stream!

We were very hungry after all the exercise.
We learned to make a campfire and then had
a cook-out lunch. It tasted great.

The walk back seemed long.
We were all very tired,
but we sang all the way home.

I can't wait until next year.
Next year my class will go on
an overnight camping trip.
We will learn about trees and lakes,
rivers and streams.
My school calls it Outdoor Education.
I think that outdoor education is the best way
to learn about nature.

Picture talk

What season of the year is it? How do you know?
Could these children use stepping stones
to cross deep water?
How have the children made sure their campfire
will not spread?

A trip to the museum

I am always getting into trouble.
I don't try to. It just happens.

Today my class went to the museum.
First we looked at the beetle display.
Then we looked at the mummies all wrapped up.
We saw china dolls, and toys of long ago.
I liked the beetles, the mummies, the dolls, and
the toys, but I could not wait to see the
dinosaur skeletons.
My teacher kept saying, "Wait a little longer,
Charles. We will be seeing the dinosaurs soon."

Just then, I peeked into the next room
and there it was, the brontosaurus,
my favorite dinosaur.
I was so excited.
I couldn't stop myself. I couldn't wait.
I ran into the next room.
Right in front of me was the enormous tail
of the great brontosaurus.
It was so big, I had to jump up to touch it.
I imagined myself riding through jungles
on the back of the brontosaurus.
I imagined adventures we could have.

Then I saw the museum guard and my teacher
coming toward me.
I remembered where I was and I knew
I was in trouble again!
Why does it always happen to me?

Picture talk

Why should you not touch exhibits at a museum?
Why do you think Charles gets into trouble?
Do you get into trouble sometimes?

After school

I'm Nathan.
When school gets out, my friend
Mona goes home.
Daniel goes to his grandmother's house.
I go to my day-care center.
My mommy and daddy work in a
big office downtown.
They can't pick me up until 6 o'clock.

Most of the time, I like being at day care.
When I arrive at the center, I have a snack
so I won't be hungry before dinner.
I play with other kids.
We make things at the art table.
We build things at the block center.
We pretend at the dress-up center.
Sometimes I like to be by myself,
so I choose something quiet to do.
I go to the reading center or the
listening center.

There are many things to do
at day care, but I am always ready to
go home at the end of the day.
I am always happy to see my mom and dad.

Picture talk

Where do you go after school?
What do you do there?
Look at all the activities in the picture.
Which one would you choose to do? Why?
Do you ever like to be alone? When?
What do you like to do when you are alone?
Where would you go if you were at this
day-care center and wanted to be alone?

26

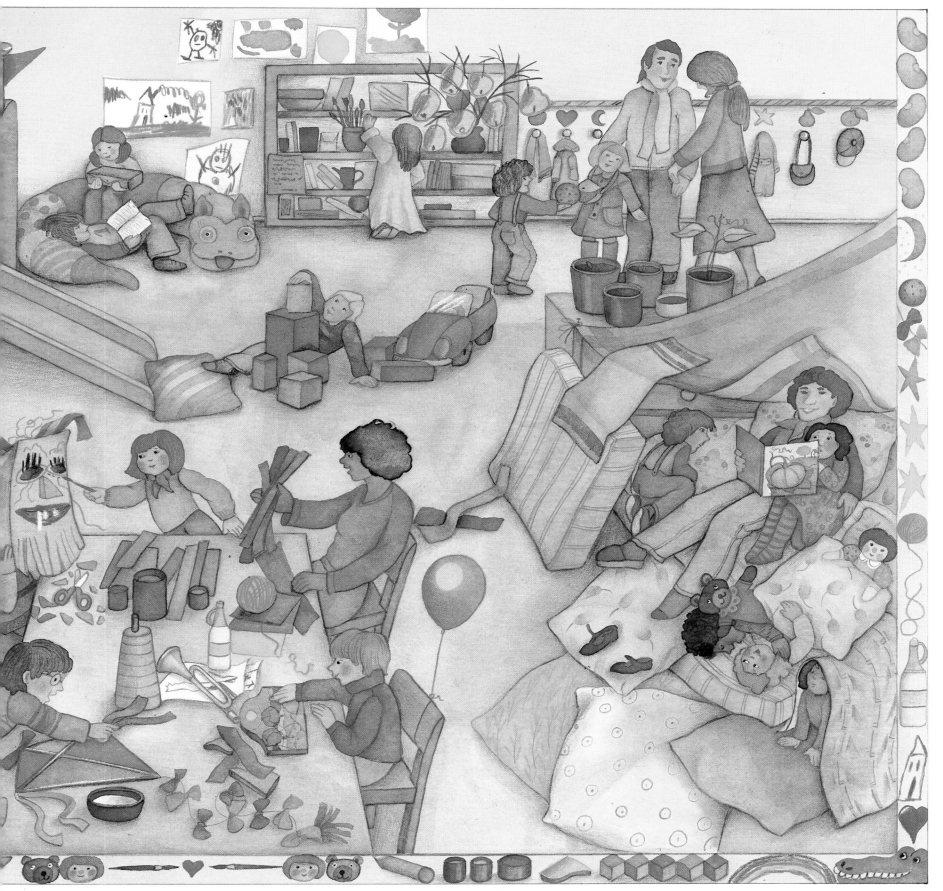

A school day

Was it hard for you to get used to a whole day at school? Did you get hungry before lunchtime? Did you get tired before the school day ended? What other things did you find hard to get used to? What would you do if the following things happened to you?

1. You are sitting at your desk and suddenly you feel very sick. Your teacher is busy with one of the reading groups. What should you do?

2. You go outside for recess. One of the kids in grade five calls you names. What can you do?

3. You and your friend have been talking. Your teacher tells you to be quiet. You go back to work but your friend keeps talking to you. What would you do?

4. You have been working hard on a picture for art. You think it is special. You are almost finished when one of your classmates comes up to you and tells you that your picture is stupid. What would you do?

Willie wants to stay home

My mom wakes me every morning at 7 o'clock.
"Time to get up for school, Willie," she calls.
Well, today I'm not going to school. I told her so.
"What do you mean you're not going to school?
You have to go to school, Willie," Mom says.
"But Mom," I said, "you don't go to work every day.
Why do I have to go to school every day?"

It's not that I don't like school.
I just don't like to go to school *every* day.
And I don't like to go *all* day.
My stomach growls for food long before
I get to eat lunch.
I like my teacher, but there are so many kids
in my class that sometimes I think
my teacher forgets about me.
I like to learn, but I can't sit at my
desk for such a long time.

Recess is my favorite part of the day.
Well, it *was* my favorite part until this big kid
from the fourth grade came along.
Whenever he sees me, he says, "Oh look,
there's Willie Nillie."
"My name is not Willie Nillie," I tell him.
"It's Willie, just plain old Willie!"
But he only looks at me with a funny grin
and goes on calling, "Willie Nillie, Willie Nillie,
Willie Nillie," until I want to scream.

As I sit at the table eating my corn flakes
with bananas on top, I remember that today is
my show-and-tell day.
I was going to bring a picture of my
new two-wheeler bicycle.
I also remember that today is the day
we're going to make dinosaurs out of clay.
I was going to make a tyrannosaurus rex.
And today is also the day I promised to play
with Leah and Jeremy at recess.
Maybe I will go to school after all.
I can always stay home tomorrow.

Later that morning...
When Mom dropped me off at school,
I lined up with the other kids.
My teacher came out to meet our class.
She looked right at me and gave me a wink!
I guess I am glad I came to school.
I think I'll probably come tomorrow.

29

Recess games
Duck, Duck, Goose

Form a circle with your friends. Hold hands. One of you is IT. That person must walk around the outside of the circle. He or she taps each friend's head, saying, "Duck, Duck, Duck..."

Finally, IT taps a friend's head and says, "Goose." Goose runs around the outside of the circle. IT runs in the other direction. The first one back to Goose's place in the circle may remain there. The other person will now be IT.

Fox and Geese

Clear a big circle in the snow with your feet. Clear six or eight lines going into the center of the circle. The snow design should look like a wheel with spokes. The person chosen to be Fox stands at the very center of the circle. The Geese run in one direction around the outside ring. Fox then chases the Geese by running down the paths which go from the center to the outside. The Goose that is caught becomes the new Fox.

Rainy day games
"Um"

One player is blindfolded. The other players sit on the floor in a circle or half circle. The blindfolded player plunks down in front of another player, and says, "Um." The seated player says, "Um" three times in a disguised voice. The blindfolded player may not touch the seated player. She must guess who the person sitting in front of her is by listening to that person's voice.

If the blindfolded player guesses correctly, the blindfold is passed on to another player. All the other players change places and the game begins again. If the player who is IT does not guess correctly, she sits in front of a different child and tries again.

Who's Missing?

Choose one person to be IT. The other players put down their heads and cover their eyes. The player who is IT very quietly taps someone on the head, who then leaves the room. IT says, "1—2—3, heads up." The children must try to guess who is hiding. When they guess correctly, the person who left the room becomes IT.

7-Up

Seven children are chosen to be IT. The other players put their heads down and cover their eyes. Each of the children who are IT taps a player on the shoulder. The children who have been tapped put a thumb up, but keep their heads down. The seven children who are IT go back to the front of the room. They say, "7-Up." The players lift their heads. The seven children who were tapped on the shoulder stand up. They each try to guess who tapped them. If a child guesses the right person, the children exchange places.

When all seven children have had a turn to guess, the game starts again. If a child does not guess the right person, a new child should be chosen to be IT.

Stoneface

All the players sit in a circle. Each player has three small pebbles or stones. The first player begins the game by trying to make the person sitting next to him laugh or smile. He can make funny faces or tell silly jokes, but no touching or tickling is allowed.

If the person laughs before two minutes is up, she must put one of her pebbles into the center of the circle. Then it is her turn to try to make the person sitting next to her laugh or smile.

The game continues until only one person is left with any pebbles. The winner is called Stoneface. Can you guess why?

Your Story

Word helpers

These words will help you to write your own story about your school.

school words
kindergarten
grade
class
reading
writing
math
science
music
field trip
library
museum
field day
outdoor education
lunch
recess

classroom words
ruler
pencil
blackboard
table
center
desk
teacher
student
eraser
book

art words
painting
molding
drawing
building
clay
paint
crayon
paper
cardboard
smock
brush
glue
scissors

action words
draw
learn
jump
skip
play
paint
mold
build
measure
count
race

123456789 BP Printed in Canada 4321098765